CUMBRIAN

by

JOHN DAWSON

COUNTRYSIDE BOOKS

NEWBURY · BERKSHIRE

First published 1997
© John Dawson 1997

COUNTRYSIDE BOOKS
3 Catherine Road
Newbury, Berkshire

ISBN 1 85306 460 2

Produced through MRM Associates Ltd., Reading
Printed by Woolnough Bookbinding Ltd., Irthlingborough

CONTENTS

The author by the door of Sir Daniel Fleming's privy, Rydal Hall.

FOREWORD

Researching the material for this book has been a fascinating exercise. I had scarcely given a thought to old privies before, but having set out along what at first I loftily described as 'this little-known byway of social history', I soon found what a big subject it is. A person could spend many years finding and recording the vast number that survive – most of them, admittedly, lacking their interior fixtures

I discovered, too, how interested in the subject most people are. I would go to a village where I was a complete stranger, following a tip-off that so-and-so still had a privy in their garden. Conversation would then reveal that old Mrs ... had one, in good condition, just along the way, and 'there will be Mr ... – he still has one' and 'what about the ...'s?' By now one or more neighbours would have joined in, and I would end up with half a dozen or more little houses to look at. Not surprising, really, because in the old days every cottage, house or farm would have one. As the work went on I became quite expert at detecting privies from a considerable distance, even to the extent of becoming a potential hazard on the road. As I was driving along, I would be liable to slow down abruptly, saying, 'Look over there – that's a good one!'

In the end, therefore, I had recorded scores of privies, enough to be able to classify them broadly and to recognise common features at a glance. Beyond a certain point I began to repeat myself, and I ended with far more photographs than I could use – but at least this meant that I didn't miss anything unusual. This also applies to the observations which I noted from so many helpful and sympathetic informants. When everyone tells you the same thing, from whatever part of the county, it looks as if you are getting the real picture.

This tremendous range of information is one reason for the

anonymity of many of my sources. When seven or eight folk from widely separated villages have mentioned the same thing, it would be invidious to write, 'as Mrs ... was able to tell me!' A further interesting point is the detached way in which everyone spoke to me. No-one gave way to long-winded or silly euphemisms – but then, most Cumbrians have been brought up in a matter-of-fact, realistic manner. The privy and its use were an inescapable part of life, to be referred to in the same sort of way as delivering a calf or castrating a lamb. Then I had to accept the force of a practical reason for not precisely identifying the whereabouts of particular farms or houses. More than most places, Cumbria is subject to massive invasions from visitors, and, as one lady put it, 'The neighbours will recognise that it's ours,' (she wasn't in the least bothered about that) 'but I don't want folk coming to the door with their cameras round their necks!'

So, my sincere thanks to everyone who volunteered information. Without their interest and co-operation, this book could never have been written. Nevertheless, there are a number of folk whose help must be acknowledged more precisely. Firstly, I must thank my wife, Margaret, for all her help on the book; Jancis Andrews and Mona Atkinson for allowing me to quote from articles which they had previously published; Audrey Dent for allowing me to include her poem; and Dr Blake Tyson for permission to quote from some of his own already published antiquarian researches. Margaret has been the official photographer, but I must also thank Peter Bibby, Marjorie Campion, Audrey Grisedale and Marcelle Upson for permission to use photographs from their own collections.

I have done my best to be accurate, and to do justice to the information and anecdotes I have been given; if there has been any misunderstanding or misinterpretation, responsibility lies with the author.

JOHN DAWSON

[1]

PRIVIES OF YESTERYEAR

There must have been privies in Cumbria for as long as people have been living in the area, but no traces of the earliest ones remain. The first recognisable installations date from Roman times. At Housesteads Fort on Hadrian's Wall, just over the border in Northumberland, the soldiers' latrines have survived, and doubtless similar structures existed at the numerous military sites within the county. Then after a break of several hundred years we come to the great castles and religious houses of the Middle Ages. In the guide books you will usually find their privies referred to as 'garderobes'. This looks like an early example of finding another word for the privy. Strictly, it means 'wardrobe', according to my dictionary; but you wouldn't keep your clean shirts and doublets in a cubby-hole containing just a stone slab, set on another vertical one, at sitting height, with a round hole cut in the middle of it.

These little rooms, built into the thickness of the walls, look draughty, cold and uncomfortable as you go round – for example – Brougham Castle near Penrith. But remember that when they were in use, there would be a wooden cover on the stone slab, and probably rushes on the floor. They were indeed superior in every respect to the facilities enjoyed by most people until quite recent times. They were incorporated on all floors of a castle – even, at Brougham, in a dungeon – so nobody had to go outside to use them. They were discreetly placed also, in such a way as ensured that a person could use them without publicity. This applies to the garrison garderobes as well as the ones in the lord's apartments. In the guard house at Brougham the privy is up three steps at the end of a passage which curves away through

This garderobe in St Mary's Priory, Carlisle, is particularly well preserved. It is said that they used to hang clothes in these places because they thought that the smell kept the moths away. (Photograph by permission of the Heritage Services Commission, Cumbria County Council)

Brougham Castle. A typical garderobe in the thickness of the wall.

Clearance hole at the foot of the garderobe chute, Coniston Hall, one of Sir Daniel Fleming's homes.

the thickness of the wall. The ventilation in all these places, too, is good; perhaps rather overdone for midwinter, but then a person wouldn't wish to stay there for a long period, and would soon be on their way back to the warmth of the fireside.

The disposal arrangements also were practical and efficient. Some of the drops, maybe, were very long, but they ran straight down to openings at the base of the exterior walls, from which the accumulation of soil could be taken away at intervals. Where external disposal was not practicable, the chutes sometimes fed into a capacious stone trough somewhere in the nether regions. I have not been able to establish whether the ash from the castle fires was mixed with the contents of the garderobes, but it seems unlikely that the practice remained undiscovered until the 16th century. The inhabitants of the great monasteries

Furness Abbey, showing the point where the great drain is divided into three channels.

Brougham Castle. An internal trough below a garderobe chute.

Drop chute into the drain below the abbot's lodging, Furness Abbey.

were not troubled by this particular problem. Not only did their austere way of life mean that there were far fewer fires to provide ash, but they tended to rely, like the Roman legionaries, on water dispersal systems for their sewage disposal.

Furness Abbey, near Barrow, is a wonderful example of the sophistication and efficiency of the monks' arrangements. They harnessed a considerable stream which runs through their valley, and at a point just above the abbey buildings, culverted the water into three separate channels – one to run beneath the abbot's lodging, one beneath the monks' latrines (known to authors of guide books as the 'reredorter'), and one beneath the great kitchen. The observant visitor to this abbey may still notice the beautifully constructed chute of dressed stone feeding into the drain below the abbot's quarters, as well as the bases of a

Bases of the three garderobes in the guest house, Furness Abbey, alongside the main drain – also including a glimpse of the drain outlet from the lay brothers' range.

The exposed garderobe at Coniston Hall, with its long drop to the clearance hole. Note the well preserved seat.

group of three garderobes which served a guest house just a few yards away. Furness is a specially good place to visit, both on account of its size and the high quality of the surviving work-manship, whether in the privies or the choir stalls – but a visit to any of our old abbeys will bring its rewards.

On a smaller scale, the gentry enjoyed the same amenities, and in a few places there is still something to be seen. Half a gar-derobe survives in the ruinous portion of Coniston Hall, seat of the le Flemings for many generations. Sir Daniel Fleming, who moved the family headquarters to Rydal in the 17th century, provides us with one of the earliest written references to the kind of privy, or earth closet, which forms the main subject of this study. In the course of his research into the buildings at Rydal Hall, Dr Blake Tyson discovered, in Sir Daniel's accounts, references to what long survived as a two-seater privy in a lean-to against the brewhouse, next to the beck. In 1673, on 2nd July, he paid eight shillings to Percy Corral's son 'for 4 load of stone lime for playstering ye closets by ye brewhouse chimney'. Later in the same summer he paid carpenters and 'ye glasiers' for further work at 'ye two closetts'.

In the course of other work on historic farm buildings, Dr Tyson unearthed a fascinating reference dating from 1798, which also shows how little the privy as we remember it changed over the centuries. Recording expenses for that year, the Head-master of Hawkshead Grammar School, the Rev T. Bowman, noted his 'disbursements for building a pigsty, Necessary and Ashes house at Knipefold'. Almost certainly this would be one of the multi-use privy buildings, noticed later in chapter 3. The use of the euphemism 'necessary' is also found in Dorothy Wordsworth's writings. On 22nd December 1801 there had been a heavy fall of snow, the sloppy kind that begins to melt almost at once. Nevertheless she and William had been out walking from their Grasmere home, and he had continued his walk when she returned to Dove Cottage. 'When he came home,' she wrote, 'he cleared a path to the necessary – called me out to see it, but before we got there a whole home-top full of snow had fallen from the roof upon the path.' Hard luck, William, but at least you had been showing willing!

The bigger houses, and indeed many smaller ones, included 'commode' chairs in their furnishings. Servants would be on hand for emptying the pails, or you trotted out with it yourself. A lady who came to visit a country-dwelling cousin told me how she would occasionally encounter her aunt in the hallway, carrying a little bucket, the purpose and significance of which it did not occur to her to question at the time. In view of the distant siting of many privies, the commode was an essential amenity for the aged or the infirm.

But Cumbrian privies in bygone days had their darker side, too, especially as the towns grew larger during the 19th century. If Kendal is taken as an example, this is not because it was worse than others, but because its problems have been so fully documented, not least by a succession of conscientious and capable Medical Officers of Health. The crux of the matter, of course, was that there were too many people in confined spaces. What was acceptable, even ecologically satisfactory, in a scattered rural area, became a terrible health hazard in an urban setting. From a Public Health Survey of 1849 we learn the reason why St Thomas's church, built in the mid-1830s, has its tower at the east end. The west end could not provide a firm enough foundation because the builders discovered a mass of solidified sewage to a depth of at least 12 feet. This stuff had percolated down over the years from the closely packed cottages higher up the hillside. Then, merely one example among many, in Moffat's Court, Stricklandgate, there were 2 privies for 35 cottages in which 120 people lived. No wonder that cholera was such a prevalent disease!

So great was the volume and complexity of the work that had to be done, that many years passed before all the old privies had been demolished. In 1886 Charles Paget, the Medical Officer of Health, drew the attention of his committee to the fact that there was still an average of more than three houses to one closet in the poorer areas of the town. His successor, Musgrave Craven, did not mince his words six years later: 'I trust the Corporation will make an earnest endeavour still further to diminish the number of midden privies, the contents of which systematically lie at the doors of the people for months at a time.' Then, acidly, in his next report: 'Now a heavy shower of rain is the only scavenger that visits the place.' Statistics from the interwar years show the authorities responding as best they could, and eventually, in 1951, references to privies cease in the reports. It wasn't lack of will that made the death of the town privy such a long drawn-out process. Problems connected with drainage and water supply that never arose on remote moorland farms were often difficult and expensive to solve. For instance, from the 1886 report again: 'W.C.'s are taking the place of privies, and the accompanying ashpits, which formerly held a year's refuse that had to be emptied in swills through the dwellings, have been filled up and ash pails substituted.'

This story could have been paralleled from the records of any other major Cumbrian town, and illustrates forcefully how important the public health services are to comfortable and civilised life.

A few sample statistics from the present century, from the Kendal Health Reports:

	Privies as only accommodation	Ashpits abolished
1922	57	19
1927	12	9

	Surviving privies, but not sole accommodation
1938	17
1949	16

The reference in the paragraph above to WCs shows how the Kendal Authorities were well abreast of the latest technological developments. It had only been in the previous decade that Thomas Crapper's Valveless Waste Preventer had been patented: 'One Moveable Part Only. Certain Flush With Easy Pull. Will Flush When Only Two-Thirds Full.' (Were these last two sentences MEANT as a rhyming couplet?) Crapper did more for the cause of public health through his invention of the water flush system than any other person. His life and work and the rapid general adoption of his invention are a subject in themselves, which lies outside the scope of this little book.

[2]

DOWN THE GARDEN PATH

Where is it, then? The answer usually is: right at the far end of the garden, orchard, paddock or yard, often incorporating a section of the property's boundary wall in its construction. Looking back to her first experience of these places as an evacuee, first near Alston, then at Nenthead, in the 1940s, Jancis Andrews commented that the landlady 'gave mother directions involving warm clothing and certain landmarks to the north and east, as if, here, you did not go to the lavatory, you emigrated to it.' The length of journey tended to vary with the size of the garden and the lie of the land, because it was desirable not only to distance the privy from the house, but also to have the ground dropping away behind the building, to make the work of clearing out rather easier. Preferably there would be room to bring a horse and cart to the site, with enough turning area to back the cart to a point within easy shovel-throw from the clearance hole. Finally, a neat little path, flagged and where needful stepped, led to the desired haven, so that on rainy days at least you didn't get your feet wet. Not that flags were the complete antidote to rain-soaking. One lady from South Lakeland shiveringly recalled how the hydrangeas planted along both sides of the path to her grandmother's little house, ensured that a small girl returned to the kitchen door with her legs cold and wet.

One privy, tucked away at the bottom of a particularly steeply sloping garden in the Vale of Newlands, was whitened for better recognition in the dark. Very occasionally the privy was situated above the house, but this was only when the distance could guarantee that downhill seepage would be prevented. A fine example, situated in Bouth, was perhaps placed there for

The whitened privy at the foot of the steps in the Vale of Newlands.

the sake of the wonderful view of the distant mountains from its door; more likely because it empties conveniently into the next-door neighour's garden. Penny Buick, new to the property, who owns this one was proposing to demolish it. However, my conversation with her led to us calling on a neighbour, whose husband had turned theirs into a garden store. One conversation led to another, and by the end of the afternoon we had found several more privies within a hundred yards of our starting point. So maybe the demolition idea is being reconsidered!

In many places, especially more public ones, the privies were built against a far corner of the boundary wall. Good examples of this arrangement include schools, places of worship and industrial sites. Sometimes it was possible to take advantage of one of those swiftly flowing becks with which Cumbria is so liberally

A two-unit privy block emptying directly into the beck, High Furness.

Down the Garden Path

Privy built directly over a beck at Tilberthwaite, and incorporating a foot-
bridge. Recently restored by the National Trust.

Privy adjoining its cottage in South Cumbria. This was feasible because the privy was built directly over a little stream which was culverted and covered for several yards with huge flags.

endowed. There are quite elaborate privies which discharge from the conventionally placed clearance hole into a stream. Others are built directly over the water. This meant that they could adjoin the house itself, thereby sparing the occupants the 30 or 40 yard pilgrimage that so many older people today remember vividly.

Grace Sloan recalled a fine three-holer at Rowrah, now demolished. I found an excellent illustration of this type of privy standing above a beck which has been culverted, with the area in front of it, outside the back door of the cottage, covered with huge stone slabs. The drawback to this kind of situation, of course, is that there are times when even sizeable becks are reduced to trickles, or dry up altogether. But there is no denying that the little house perched like a tiny bridge over the stream is exceedingly picturesque.

Jean Stephens, like Grace Sloan, from Lamplugh, told me how one of these water-cleared privies came to be constructed within living memory. The village joiner-cum-undertaker was officially required to provide toilet facilities for his workmen. The youngest apprentice (now an old man) was told to make a wooden board with two holes of suitable diameter cut in it. Then he had to fix two stout planks across the nearby stream, and set his board on top of them. This sounds very like the way they used to dig a big hole on a building site, and then put planks across it! There was no mention of the apprentice making a sheltering superstructure or screening fence. Nevertheless, it was not uncommon, especially in the northern part of Cumbria, for the privy to be screened by a beech, or other thick and sturdy, hedge. This was fine, except that it added to the darkness during winter visits, and made it more essential than ever to take a candle, oil lamp or torch.

These hedged privies were by no means confined to sites where the number of neighbouring houses perhaps suggested a

25

need for greater seclusion. One informant recalled a remote farm on the side of one of our western fells. The privy was some way from the house, beyond the farm buildings and on a small plot enclosed by a high hedge, and it stood right on the very edge of a stream. 'It must have come from a spring on the fell,' he wrote. 'As far as I remember, it never ran dry. The water swirled in and out so that it was always clean and never needed emptying.' And think of the superb ventilation!

This contribution gives substance to Mrs Andrews' remark about 'emigrating' to the lavatory, and, indeed, the farms provided the most exciting privy runs. Sometimes it was a straight dash across the yard, with no worse hazard than a stray cowpat. To quote Mrs Andrews again: 'Mother made me put on my coat and led me out ... She waded through a sea of cowpats surging

Exterior of a privy near Ulverston, showing how it fits snugly against the barn wall and how soundly constructed it is.

Exterior of rare brick-built privy not far from Ravenglass, showing position against barn wall, in garden but handy to house.

Door to the privy inside the big barn at Jackson Ground, Broughton Mills. Note the clearance hole on the right.

around the hand pump that was the only source of (pure?) drinking water, and kept turning corners until we reached the barn. The lavatory proved to be a stone outhouse presently occupied by a large cow, obviously ambitious to be toilet-trained. Nearby was the herd, looking as threatening to life and limb as a battalion of Sherman tanks.' One farmer that I met on my travels, Mr R. Robinson of Jackson Ground, Broughton Mills, made a great point of keeping the door firmly shut, or cows and hens would go inside. My researches have also taken me to places where you would have to cross a rough yard, turn down an uneven slope beyond a barn, then make your way between the barn and the high stone wall of a sheep pen to the dark and dismal installation at the end of the journey.

Such privies were often built as a lean-to against the barn

Fairly recent pairs of privies serving a row of quarrymen's cottages at Holme Ground, Tilberthwaite. Rear view; note openings into central ashpits.

wall, a practice to be found throughout Cumbria, and not confined to a particular period. A very well-preserved brick structure I found was erected in this style relatively recently, and probably as an up-to-date modernisation. Rarely, there was a privy within one of the big barns, right at one end, where the outlet was conveniently close to the farm midden.

Then in settlements linked to older villages where the 19th-century mining and quarrying boom had led to new building in the neighbourhood, the privies were often quite imposing structures. Typically they were in pairs, not too far from the row of cottages they served, doors facing the row, and at the back, clearance holes and access to the central ashpit which separated the two privy units. Sometimes there was a privy block at the end of a long row of cottages, where the constricted or steep nature of

A row of cottages frequently had a privy block at some distance from one end. This block, situated in the Coppermines Valley above Coniston, has the most spectacular setting of any of the privies I encountered.

the site prevented the more spacious arrangement. By contrast, one such block took advantage of a small stream in the wide spaces of Coppermines Valley, Coniston and thereby became perhaps the most spectacularly sited set of privies in the entire county.

All the examples quoted above are to be found in the rural parts of Cumbria. Their equivalents, which had to serve the often overcrowded central areas of our towns in the years before piped water became general and Thomas Crapper's invention commonplace, were nearly always so unsatisfactory and formed such a serious public health hazard that they have all been swept away.

[3]

PRIVY DESIGN

There must be hundreds of privy buildings throughout Cumbria, most of them in good repair, although not many retain their internal fittings. Once you start to look, you see them in the gardens of nearly all the old and not-so-old houses because before the days of mains water the earth closet was for most people the only option. They are easy to pick out, since the usual term for them – the small house – is so apt.

Generally the privy was constructed of the local stone, well proportioned, and the gabled roof covered with local slate. The little house was made to last as long as what may be described as its parent. Indeed the character of the stone and the style of construction shows that many date back at least as far as the great rebuilding of Cumbrian farms in the 17th and 18th centuries. A rough guide to dating is to see whether the stone has been dressed. No sign of dressing usually indicates a great age; sawn stone means quite a late date, possibly a reconstruction. The only criticism about the design today would have to come from tall persons, who would find the doorway too low; but a high door would have spoiled the proportions, and it would have been a waste of effort and resources to make the whole building needlessly high. Anyway, the bumps would quickly teach a taller than average person to bend.

The overall size of the privy varied in direct ratio to the establishment which it served. The little cottage model needed to accommodate no more than a single hole internally; the general purpose farm model was rather bigger, featuring two holes. Then there were architect designed installations for the mansion or small country house. These were often divided by a central

A very old farm privy not far from Coniston. A section of it was probably once partitioned off as a dog hut.

The family/staff privy block at one of our bigger houses in a small, remote valley. Note the garden setting and the external dividing wall.

interior wall, thus providing for the family at one end and staff, particularly perhaps those whose work was mainly in the grounds, at the other. A head-high external wall would further separate the sheep from the goats and maintain a degree of privacy for anyone approaching or leaving. A variation on this pattern was to have a door on one of the longer sides, with a hedge or bushes screening the approach from the house, and another door in the gable wall reached along an open path or by means of a short flight of stone steps.

One farm which I visited, overlooking Coniston Water, boasted no fewer than three privies. The oldest one, across the yard from the original house, was of the dual-purpose type and quite large. Both house and privy were almost certainly well over 400 years old. At a much later date a new farmhouse – plus a cottage – was built onto the end of the old dwelling to form, roughly, a letter T. This now gave a handsome and well-proportioned front looking onto a piece of garden ground. Then, later still, perhaps because the original privy was obviously inadequate to meet the needs of the occupants (the farm in question has a long association with the Lake District tourist industry), two extra privies were set up, one at each end of the newer building. They were at a short distance from the garden-facing front, to which they were joined by a length of high stone wall, pierced on either side of the house by an archway. This wall formed one side of the half-gabled privy, which was thus entirely concealed from the garden, but easily accessible from either the front or the back of the house. The overall effect is delightful, recalling the way in which classically designed stately homes sometimes have a detached pavilion linked by a wall to the

Near Great Asby. Go across the yard and you will find this half-gabled privy facing onto the garden.

corners of the front elevation of the house.

The half-gabled style of privy building usually seems to have been dictated by the nature of the site. In later years it lent itself more readily to the use of corrugated iron, but so well were the original roofs constructed that examples are very rare. Stone was also the favoured material, in the shape of a big flag, to block the outside clearance hole, although here again a large sheet of metal was an occasional alternative. All the constructional details of the small houses were well finished. The clearance hole, for example, would have a good stone lintel, the corners of the walls were held in place by big quoin stones, and the apex of the roof capped by proper ridge tiles.

Some of these privies are very pretty little buildings today, festooned with hanging baskets, or with roses or jasmine round the door. Probably they were less frequently so garlanded in the old days. Everyone would have plenty of work to do without turning the privy into a flowery bower, although there is evidence that the owners of some of the bigger houses took care that the approach at least was pleasantly landscaped. Not that the privy invariably lent itself to prettification. The old dual-purpose one at Coniston Water almost certainly housed dogs or a pig, separated by a partition wall from the temporary human occupants. Another such, near Great Asby, has a finely preserved opening in the gable wall, opposite the privy end, through which it was possible to post food to the pig. The swill dropped into a convenient trough below without a person having to open the door and physically go inside every feeding time.

Some of the small houses were multi-functional. There was a pig sty (or pig hole as it was often called) at one end, to which was joined a small exercise yard, its wall topped by level flagstones. The privy was at the other end of the building. Then, in the roof space above the pig hole, with access through a sort of trap door from the privy, was accommodation for birds. Generally these

The steps up to the staff section of a family/staff privy block in South Cumbria.

Entrance to the family section. Note the discreetly sited shrub.

The 'balancing' pair of privies at opposite ends of the garden frontage at a
farm overlooking Coniston Water. Note how they are built against the
ornamental wall.

Back wall of the privy on a remote fell farm above Millom, showing how it was slotted between the barn and the sheep pen. Clearance hole blocked with a flagstone.

A disused privy can be made into an attractive element in the whole design of a garden, as here in the Rusland Valley. This is an old cottage privy – note the lowness of the doorway.

were hens, which could roost there safe from foxes and come out in the daytime via their own little hatch, from which provision was made for them to hop down to the flat wall top surrounding the pig sty. At Jackson Ground game cocks were confidently identified as the former tenants of this roof space; and at another farm, pigeons, which formerly provided a welcome source of fresh meat. In the course of his researches into Cumbrian farm buildings, Dr Blake Tyson has also discovered examples of this unusual arrangement in Long Sleddale and Kentmere – one with pig pen, roof space for hens and cantilevered stone steps for them to go up and down; another, even more versatile, attached to the gable wall of a barn, which included a dog kennel in its accommodation. It has to be said that whilst an attic roost may have been fine for the hens, it was less than ideal for the person

A different view of the privy at Great Asby. This end may have been the pig
hole; food could be posted through the little opening in the wall to fall into a
trough beneath..

standing tiptoe on the privy board trying to reach the far corners
when cleaning out. A variant on this multipurpose privy unit
may be seen where the privy and the pig sty are side by side as
parts of a longer building situated at the edge of the yard, but
handily close to the general midden.

If a small brick structure is identified as a privy it is almost
certainly quite new. Sometimes these are to be seen at the
bottom of the yard in semi-urban places where houses were
built for railway workers, perhaps, or miners, or in association
with public buildings like schools. So great has been the scale of
demolition or modernisation that these are not easily found;
nevertheless a few survive, where a school has been closed and
the site has not been redeveloped. The one illustrated, at
Torver, is as ugly as the majority of the old stone ones are attrac-

41

General view of the little house at Whinfell, Grayrigg. The pig and the poultry at the end nearer the camera, the privy at the far end.

tive in appearance. Side by side, one for the boys and one for the girls, with what was doubtless the teachers' one at the other side of the ashpit. By contrast, at a Quaker meeting house near Hawkshead they had been more thoughtful in keeping a decent space between the facilities provided for the different sexes. The women's privy, stone of course, was situated completely out of sight of the one reserved for the men. Elsewhere, one spacious brick privy was found set against the gable wall of an old barn, and seemed quite out of character with its surroundings. Closer examination showed the outline on the barn wall, a little farther along, of the gabled roof line of what must have been the original privy. It is highly unlikely that this would have fallen down, so I concluded that the brick replacement was an illustration of installing something more up to date, and perhaps thereby

The small house at Jackson Ground, Broughton Mills. Mr Robinson still keeps dogs on the ground floor, but draws the line at game cocks, which once occupied the 'cockloft' above.

A splendid multi-purpose building at a National Trust farm in Yewdale. Note the steps up to the granary, the access door to the ashpit-midden next to the steps, the privy door with its tiny window and the door into the pig hole.

keeping a step ahead of the neighbours.

It should not be assumed that all the discoverable privies are going to be ancient. Some places, even in the villages, still have no connection with the public drainage system. They rely on chemical toilets, with which visitors to some of our campsites will be familiar. These modern privies are anything but gems of vernacular architecture – and some turn up in unexpected places. Within the curtilage of a Methodist chapel there is a 'Portaloo' discreetly concealed at the back of the building. I have also found little wooden sentry boxes (hardly houses!) both at isolated farms and at temporary bases for outdoor organisations far from normal habitations. There are even a few traditional earth closets still in regular use, so the Cumbrian privy is still alive – if not exactly flourishing.

Modern privy still in regular use at the Methodist chapel in one of our larger villages.

Modern privy at an outdoor activities hut hidden among the fells above Derwentwater.

General view of the privies in the corner of the yard at the former primary school, Torver. The staff privy was in the farther part of the building, and emptied into the same midden.

Disposal tank at one of the bigger campsites (Park Coppice).

47

[4]

LAMPS, WHITEWASH AND TWICERS

Having observed the situation of our privy from the security of the kitchen window, and then noted its external features while walking along the path through the garden, we have now reached the door of the little house itself and are almost in a position to examine its interior fixtures and fittings. But first of all, the door. If it is an old one, it is likely to have one or more tasteful diamond or heart-shaped ventilation or spy holes cut into the planking roughly at eye level; and it will not fit very well. There will be a space at either the top or the bottom several inches in extent.

Mona Atkinson, new to privies when she moved to a farm near Ulverston, speculated whether the holes were for prospective customers to peer in, or for the sitting tenant to peer out. Her next shock was to discover that there was no means of fastening the door securely shut. Indeed, there are very few with any kind of bolt on the inside; but the protective feature is that privy doors always open inwards. So Mrs Atkinson's ploy if she heard someone approaching, was to thrust her foot hard against the door and hiss 'I'm in here.' 'At first,' she writes, 'I'd try and disguise my voice so they wouldn't guess it was me, but I soon realised the futility of that; the impatient caller would only lurk round the corner waiting for me to come out. Later I discarded such modesty and even became brazen enough to give a running commentary — "Shan't be long now", or, rather sadistically, "I've only just come in, you'll have to wait".' But she found the strain of keeping one foot at the ready to repel invaders was just too much, and decided to do something about it. So she called at the ironmonger's in the nearby market town and asked for one of

Roses round the door at Haws Bank. (Photo courtesy of Audrey Grisedale)

those VACANT/ENGAGED devices that are commonly seen on the cubicle doors of public lavatories. The ironmonger was predictably sorry, he'd never been asked for one of them before, and didn't know where he could get one. But ever helpful, in the manner of country tradesmen, he suggested a card that could be hung outside on the latch. Then both judgement and good taste deserted him, as he went on to say the card could have 'GUESS WHO' printed on it ... At this point Mrs Atkinson gave up, amidst his unseemly guffaws, and made the best of living with the native traditions.

So, having discreetly made certain that no-one is in occupation, we will push the door open. Almost always the floor will be flagged. One or two avant-garde modernisers have had concrete laid down; one or two with pretensions to gentility have invested in a piece of oilcloth (or, more likely reused the best piece when last the kitchen was redone); and one of the real gentry, I discovered, had quarry tiles. The concrete would be the least satisfactory of these options, on account of the difficulty of washing it properly, though nowadays, of course, an invisible sealant would prevent dust from rubbing off. The walls will be plastered and usually whitewashed, but again, the eccentric or the better-off would buck the trend, and I have seen colourwash in a variety of shades – most often ochre or cream, but obviously there had also been times when father was using up the paint left over from a previous job.

Quite apart from ventilation supplied by the skimpy door and up from the clearance hole, the wall will be pierced with one or two tiny, unglazed openings, most often somewhere near the apex of the gable. Occasionally, and less attractively, land drainage tiles will have been incorporated in the wall. In addition, there is likely to be a tiny window, maybe only nine inches or so in its dimensions. Roof lights are very rare, mainly, no doubt, for sound constructional reasons. Fitting one into a small

Interior of the privy at Whinfell, Grayrigg.

Interior of a privy near Farleton. Note recess in the wall on the right.

Sitting tenant. (Photo courtesy of Marjorie Campion, Great Asby)

slate roof would be tricky, apart altogether from the ongoing problem of so maintaining it that rainwater never leaked in, to the additional discomfort of the occupant. But the windows were very small wherever they were, and the glazing was of the kind rather contemptuously described to me as 'hen-house glass'.

Just as important as the window was the little recess that you will nearly always see in the thickness of the wall, about three or four feet above the floor. This would be nine inches to a foot in height, and correspondingly wide and deep. The most obvious use for it was as a shelf to put your candle or lamp on when you had safely negotiated the way, and to dispel the pitch blackness of a January evening. Some folk kept a little paraffin lamp in the privy, of the kind we used to call kelly lamps; they were weighted at the base and very difficult to knock over. During the dark

Interior of the now disused family section of a privy in South Cumbria. Note the step up to the smaller hole for the children.

weather this lamp would be filled with enough fuel to last until say, 11 o'clock, and lit at dusk each day. No doubt its tiny gleam would show through the gap underneath the door, making a kind of lighthouse beam. Or the recess could hold the neatly cut newspaper squares, although these were generally threaded on a string and then hung on a convenient nail. Whole newspapers or magazines were piled at one end of the seating board frankly as reading matter. Who has never visited a house where a small section of the library is situated in the loo? Two hundred years and more ago, the great Lord Chesterfield advised his son never to waste his time idly in the privy, but to occupy himself in reading the Latin poets, with whose works he would thereby become effortlessly familiar. We have come across no authenticated example of the works of classical authors being stored in Cumbrian privies. One lady, however, recalls the frustration she felt when reading the contents of the top square on the string if the news item or feature had been cut off at a crucial point.

The essential element in the interior remains to be described. There will be a stone slab set up right across the little house, abutting on two of the available sides, most frequently opposite the door. This frontal slab will be faced, in more expensively appointed installations, by a wooden panel, which may even be elegantly decorated. One such gave equal treatment to both family and staff, with wooden skirting boards to boot. Fitted against the walls, and resting on top of this frontal stone, will be the seating board complete with hole, or holes. In a two-holer, one will normally be smaller than the other, and may well have a little step fixed against the frontal below it, so that young children, or perhaps arthritic grandparents, could reach the throne more easily. Three-holers are fairly rare; but here also the size of the holes was graduated. Several correspondents have described this set-up as 'for Father Bear, Mother Bear and Baby Bear'.

The interior of this family privy was colourwashed. Note the square, hinged lids.

Very rarely there were four- or even five-holers. Describing a four-holer that he had known, one quarryman used the three bear mantra, then added unexpectedly, 'and one for t'toads to come up. Everybody used to call that farm Toad Hall.' I have met no success in trying to unravel this mystery.

The holes were generally circular, with typical diameters of ten inches and eight inches. Occasionally the hole was more oval, with the longer axis running from front to back. Lids were not an invariable feature; or maybe in some places they have not survived. They could be loose, or hinged, on no discernible principle based either on location in the county or the apparent wealth of the former owners of the property. Possibly, however, the oval or pear shaped ones were more favoured by the gentry. In the visitors' privy at one farm guesthouse there was one circular and one oval hole, described by a representative of the present generation of the family as 'the men's and the women's'. Slate lids were not unknown, but they must have been heavy and unpleasant to handle in winter. The commonest type of seat cover was the substantial square wooden one, with two hinges. Circular lids could only take a single hinge and had to fit their hole accurately. Many circular lids were, so to speak, free-sitting.

The difference in hole sizes is an important feature. The user selected his or her most appropriate perch, and the smallness of the Baby Bear hole was a significant safety precaution. Small children could, and not infrequently did, jack-knife down into the depths if the hole was too big. 'They were always doing it!' said one correspondent, in the sort of tone that suggested she herself probably had a dreadful memory of having to be rescued. This, of course, is an argument against having any kind of lock on the door. The number of seating places, then, is not an indication that visiting the privy was a social occasion. The exception, perhaps, was a pair of sisters accompanying each other for

'There's plenty of room . . .'

security on dark nights, when the owls were crying and nameless creatures rustling among the dead leaves; or simply, if they came from a big family crowded into a small cottage, to find a place where they could talk to each other in peace and quietness for a few minutes.

I have had two stories about dual occupancy and both concerned holiday visitors at a time when earth closets were unknown in big towns but still constituted the sole available sanitation on the 'bed and breakfast' farms. One involved a young chap on his first visit. He told the farmer's wife afterwards how he had pushed open the door unthinkingly, to find another chap enthroned. He was about to retreat in embarrassed confusion, mumbling an apology, when the other said brightly, 'Oh! don't worry. There's plenty of room' – and indicating the smaller hole with a wave of his hand, went on, 'It's a twicer, you see.' 'Twicer' forthwith entered the private vocabulary of this farming family to describe a two-holer. The other story was also passed to a farmer's wife, Betty Birkett, then living at Watendlath, this time by a lady visitor, who after the initial shock had seen the funny side of the incident. She was seated on the throne, when a small boy belonging to another visiting family burst in, as small boys will. 'You can't come in here,' she had said; but he cut her short at once. 'Yes, I can,' he exclaimed, 'There's another hole here.'

The remaining essential feature was the clearance opening. Sometimes this was linked with a specially constructed pit, but the general practice was to have a movable stone slab, so that the contents could be raked out, or the hidden pail removed. And at this point the significance of the bucket and small shovel that we noticed on the floor behind the door becomes apparent. The bucket contained ash from the fire, and whenever you had used the privy, you emptied some of the ash into the depths. The reason was that the ash absorbed some of the more liquid

59

Clearance hole adjoining the midden at the rear of a farm privy. Note the flagstone used to block the hole.

contents, and gradually bound the waste confined below into a consistency that made the job of emptying and then spreading over the fields more manageable.

Having scattered our ashes, so to speak, we will withdraw to make way for the next visitor, commenting only on one or two unusual points. Peter Park remembers staying at one of the remoter Youth Hostels, Wasdale, many years ago. He would cheerfully have led you along any of the trickier rock climbing routes, but recalls with a shudder how he had to sit on a sort of open platform, quite public, perched above a long, sheer drop to the rocks below. Then, in some of the villages, where two houses shared one of those semi-detached structures or there was a row of 'netties' crowded together, things were not wholly satisfactory. As Mrs Andrews soon found out, the thin partition wall allowed neighbours 'to eavesdrop on one another's efforts'. But at least the wooden bench that she sat on had only one hole, and that right in the centre.

[5]

SPOTLESS PRIVIES

The overwhelming weight of personal recollection is that the privy was almost invariably clean and odour-free. A number of correspondents also made the point that they have no memories of suffering from 'tummy bugs'. But there was a price to be paid for achieving this cleanliness in the amount of regular hard work that had to be done. The wooden bench was scrubbed white as a butcher's chopping board; the floor and steps were regularly mopped as part of the routine of weekly household chores. And we must remember that the buckets of water needed for the work had to be carried from the pump or the slopstone in the kitchen. 'Down the steps, across the path, then up more steps,' said one lady feelingly. Elsie Youdell was more direct: 'It was quite a walk up the garden. It was horrible. I used to hate it.' But I am certain that the place was spotless after she had done her work.

Most people took a great pride in the state of their privies. 'Scrubbed and spotlessly clean' were the words used by a lady, like Elsie, from South Lakeland, recalling childhood visits to her grandmother. Granny had recently had an inside WC installed, but would not allow the grandchildren to use it, except in very special circumstances – maybe when they were paying a formal visit, wearing their Sunday clothes, and the rain was coming down in stair-rods. 'We used to tiptoe in,' she said, 'and were so careful to leave everything as bright and shining as we found it. I felt I should run my handkerchief over the seat before I left.' Fortunately, none of the children regarded it as a slight that they had to go to the little house up the garden – 'it was very nice, really, quite cosy, and anyway, it was like what we were accustomed to at home.'

The Farleton Packet. In the now ruined privy, hidden under the bushes, young Tobias Atkinson saw the writing on the wall.

In the country districts, at any rate, the owners of more public buildings seem to have made the effort to maintain at least an acceptable standard of hygiene. Tobias Atkinson, brought up at Holme and whose work took him around the county a good deal, could not recall any that were badly kept and chuckled as he told us of the Farleton Packet. This building, now roofless, may still be seen a field's distance from the M6 motorway. It is situated by the Farleton basin on the Lancaster to Kendal canal. Here barges were regularly loaded with limestone, and for many bargees it was a convenient overnight stopping place. The privy block is now no more than a heap of stones hidden beneath bushes and briars, but in the 1930s it was still very much in use and the management had set up, in the form of a graffito on the wall, the following admonitory verse:

If in this place you enter
To part with what you eat
Please put it in the centre
And not upon the seat.

If Mother Bear usually had to take responsibility for the day-to-day cleaning, Bear junior, especially if female, had to see to the paper. Quantities of newspaper had to be cut neatly into squares – one little girl, as she then was, had to make sure that the squares had ten inch sides. Then, after piercing them with a big needle, she threaded them on a piece of string so that they could hang from a nail in the back of the door. 'My job,' said Edith Bowness from Langdale, 'on a Saturday was to cut up the *News Chronicle* ready for the next week.' A family got used to its own kind of newspaper – others spoke nostalgically of the Saturday sporting papers, or the *Radio Times*, and one household swore by the *Financial Times*. One wonders what the meticulous ten by ten families did when it came to disposing of the offcuts. This problem did not arise for the labour saving families who put the early mail-order catalogues into the privy, for a person to tear off a page as required. A bonus would be the bright and cheerful character of the reading matter they provided. Really canny folk, with an eye to comfort in use, put aside all the little squares of soft tissue paper in which Christmas oranges, for example, used to be wrapped.

A big family or a guesthouse would need a fair quantity of suitable paper to last through a week. Indeed, one sad story which was told to me was of a young girl at her first position in 'service'. On Christmas morning her mistress despatched her with a pile of newspapers, scissors and string to the orchard, to make sure there was an adequate supply for the expected family gathering. And she wept all the time she was working as she thought of her own family and the Christmas she was missing.

Peter Bibby, to whom the reward of a glass of whisky was no good.

Generally one of the men would undertake the regular whitening or lime washing of the interior walls. And more often than not it was Father Bear who riddled the accumulated ash from yesterday's fire each morning. The cinders were recycled and the ashes went into the ashpit or the privy bucket. The purpose of the ash was partly to smother any unpleasant smells, but also, having mingled with the organic waste, to bind it together in an even consistency. If the privy served a farm, the farmer or one of his men dealt with the job of clearing out. He had a shovel and a 'corrack', or cowrake, what we called a muck rake in south-east Lancashire. This is a big-toothed rake with a very long handle, which was used to drag manure off the cart into heaps along the field ready for spreading with a fork. So, having leaned your tools against the wall, you backed up the empty cart to a handy distance, and raked and shovelled away for dear life. One former farmhand, Peter Bibby from Cartmel, now into his eighties, remembered how he was given this task as being the youngest and newest workman. 'They gave you a glass of whisky when you'd done,' he said. But it still rankled, as he continued, 'That was no good to me. I was teetotal – still am! ' My researches turned up very few of the cesspit type of clearance, which required the use of a long handled scoop.

Often a farmer would have a kind of 'privy round', emptying installations as the owners called him in. You paid, perhaps, sixpence, and the day when the cart arrived was something of an occasion. 'We children would look out for him,' said Edith Bowness, 'then, shouting "Here he comes", we would escort him to the little house. As he left, we would run behind, chanting "Violets! Sweet violets!" ' Or it may have been the Council midden man, whom Audrey Dent, brought up near Appleby, remembers as Tom. 'Whenever he was due to call we were very cautious about using the privy, in case we were inside when he arrived.' Wise, if the Langdale informant is to be believed who told me that anyone unlucky enough to be in occupation at the critical time was liable to receive a friendly pat on the bum from a mucky shovel. Jancis Andrews recalls another Tom, who came once a week, driving his horse and cart, piled high with the malodorous offerings of other families. 'Tom would remove your bucket via a little door at the back of the nettie, then dump the contents into his cart. A cheerful man, who had obviously developed a soul of granite as a defence against his occupation, he could be heard coming a mile away, singing hymns at the top of his voice. (On the other hand, maybe the hymns were his way of praying to God to save him from being a midden man.)'

The use of a bucket under the privy seat became much the commoner arrangement in the later years of the privy era. They made emptying easier, but the job had to be done more frequently. Undoubtedly some of the older houses among 'Tom's' ports of call must have been distinctly unappetising. Vera Grindrod from Tilberthwaite told me about his regular visits to her parents' combined privy/ashpit, into which ashes and domestic refuse were added through a smallish door, to mix haphazardly with the offerings from the privy. The only access to this dismal hole was through the door, and Tom had to leap down somehow with his shovel, and then send everything up several feet into tubs outside. His calls, fortunately, were sufficiently regular for the ordure not to spill over the tops of his wellies. 'He was only a little man, too,' said our informant: 'At the time I didn't think what an awful job it must have been – and the wooden ashpit door was ideal for playing "two balls". I was quite good at that.' So it's an ill wind ... And at the general tip to which Tom took his cargo, you could see tomato plants growing each summer.

For a farmer to have the local school on his list must have provided an excellent supply of raw material. The grandfather of one farmer near Broughton in Furness (still working the same land) would bring his horse every Monday evening, and tow away the iron troughs in which the waste had been deposited – no doubt early enough in the morning for them to have been returned by the time school opened! Mr W. McKinney, now of Bulawayo but brought up in the area between Silloth and Abbeytown, tells how every three or four weeks his father took the horse and cart to school. This was a larger establishment, and there was a bank of three or four toilets for each sex. An unpleasant job, he admits, but the young lad found some compensation in the joy of taking a ride on the cart pulled by their huge Clydesdale. 'The 'night soil' went straight on to the field near the railway, the cart was washed and tomorrow was another day.'

Occasionally a local carter or coal merchant would undertake this work, and for these contractors it was particularly important to wash the cart before starting on the next non-privy work. One classic tale in this connection concerns the carter who regularly took his cart down to Coniston Water to do this job. It was a summer evening, and the weather had been dry, so that the level of the lake was low. Now this lake shelves gradually over small stones for some distance beyond the normal water line, then falls away abruptly to a great depth. Our carter, backing into the water according to his usual practice, backed that little bit too far, and lost his cart in the deeps. Local tradition has it that somehow the cart was subsequently recovered, but is silent as to whether the horse was between the shafts when the mishap took place.

The few instances of Mother Bear taking charge of the emptying relate to the pail system. One lady from the north of the county told me that her mother always undertook this chore, even, she remembered, when she had to go into hospital the next day; and then, when she was back at home, this was the first thing she did. Her procedure was to dig a hole in the garden to receive the contents of the pail. An unsurprising consequence of this was that neighbours and visitors commented that 'we had some of the best daffodils in Cumberland!' Then I heard about the farmer's wife at a Lakeland guest house who emptied the privies personally after everyone else had gone to bed, so that none of the guests should ever see the sordid practical details of the sewage disposal. In fact her timing had good historical precedent. Thomas Tusser, compiling his *500 Points of Good Husbandry* in the mid-16th century, included 'cleansing of privies' in his list of jobs for November, thus:

> Foule privies are now to be cleansed and fide,
> Let night be appointed such baggage to hide;
> Which buried in garden, in trenches alowe,
> Shall make very many things better to growe.

To fide is a now obsolete word meaning to cleanse, so our versifier is simply saying the same thing twice in order to obtain his rhyme. A kind of Twicer!

The lady who grew wonderful daffodils was only doing the same thing as the farmers had for generations, but on a smaller scale. Our teetotal friend, Peter Bibby, made much the same point – 'we had mangolds as big as footballs.' The 'night soil' went straight on the fields – on the 'green crops' – and it was best if it could be spread on a wet day, so that the rain would dilute the tendency that excessive acidity might have to burn. The farms of the earth closet era were more mixed than most of them are today, with, often, a considerable area devoted to arable cultivation, so that extra fertilizer for these green crops was specially valued. Not that all the farm workers co-operated as wholeheartedly as they might have done. The story (Peter Bibby again) is probably not peculiar to Cumbria of the man

Clearance openings (Monk Coniston). Note nearness to beck for easy disposal of contents.

who would use the farm privy only in a dire emergency. The reason? Not his remarkable fastidiousness, but a concern to benefit his own rhubarb and leeks as much as possible.

The privies which cleared into a beck, therefore, were seldom associated with a farm. But for the householder concerned this kind was almost trouble-free. If you discharged directly into the beck, or near enough to allow a good swill out whenever there was a spate, you never needed to bother Tom.

As ever, the towns told a different story. What was every-body's convenience was nobody's responsibility. Hence the dreadful reports of pools of sewage mixed with the effluent from slaughterhouses, stables or pigsties. In one case, at Kendal, we read how in the 1840s an open sewer discharged its contents into the street gutter, which also took effluent from more houses at the end of the Market Place. All this then flowed through the cellar of an inn by way of a trough three feet wide and walled up to almost the same height at the sides . . .

[6]

PRIVIES FOR TODAY

What has been the fate of all these little houses, then? They were well designed for their purpose, and stoutly built, some of them over 300 years ago. Many of the survivors have been converted to other uses by owners who, if they care nothing for good examples of vernacular architecture, know a useful little building when they see one. Scores of them have been turned into storage accommodation for garden equipment. With the 'innards' removed, they will take quite big, unwieldy things, perhaps a wheelbarrow or a grasscutter, which come to no harm in the dry, well ventilated environment. Or, you can fill them with a huge quantity of the assorted material (a polite phrase for junk) that a garden always seems to attract – that half empty bag of peat, those plastic sacks that may come in handy one day, the fork with a bent tine, and so on and so on. Some people just stuff everything inside as occasion arises; others have precisely spaced hooks on the roof timbers, nails in the walls, and smaller things piled neatly on top of the larger ones.

In places where perhaps Father Bear is the dominating influence, the privy has become a tool shed. These are almost invariably tidy, and some have the character of a small workshop – a bench where the seating used to be, duckboard on the floor, the walls hidden behind battens and shelves loaded with the workman's specialised equipment. Electricity has even been brought to a select few, so that they are habitable on cold, dark evenings, when Father Bear wants to finish making that Christmas present for one of his children (or grandchildren), or just get away from the television.

A scattering of privies have been reused for less interesting,

Interior of privy at Coniston Water, now used as a beer store.

Privy perched above a beck near Coniston, and very much in use as a garden store.

more mundane purposes, but no less valuable to the householder concerned. If they are not too far from the back door, they make ideal wood stores or kindling sheds – again reflecting the person-alities of their owners. In one woodshed, the door of which was shining with new paint, the contents were ranged round the walls in groups of exactly the same length, set at precisely the same angle, and placed the same number of millimetres apart. Coal sheds are another kind of reuse, to which former ashpits readily lent themselves. Then the now obsolete adjacent privy could be taken over for storing the domestic clutter that we can't readily find a place for, yet are reluctant to throw away. And for folk living in small old cottages, spare space within the home is often hard to find. These 'storeroom' privies are gener-ally very well maintained, with cement render on the walls and a

Privy converted to garden shed, Bouth.

stout, close-fitting door which locks securely.

Not all conversions are so utilitarian. One that I saw, not far from Ulverston, has been turned into a delightful little summer house, set in a pretty and lovingly tended garden. Numbers of others, maybe with some gardening tackle inside, have been consciously made into gardening features – a sort of homely version of the classical temples that we see in the grounds of stately homes. Especially when they are at some distance from the house, they can become a focal point in the vista. This kind are apt to have roses round the door, or hanging baskets fixed to the wall alongside the door lintel. But care is needed here – after all, the house is small, by definition, and heedless rampant climbing plants can virtually obliterate the shape and features of the building.

Privy building next to a National Trust cottage in South Lakeland.

Privy converted to delightful summer house, Bouth.

Few privies were big enough to be turned satisfactorily into hen cotes, but the owners of one or two larger specimens have done so at different times. One of the 'over-beck' privies in South Lakeland served in this capacity for years. A movable cover on the clearance hole prevented the untimely loss of any of the hens, and rendered the job of cleaning the place remarkably easy. Sometimes the poultry claimed possession of a whole building in which originally they had been confined to the roof space. Anyway, keeping a few hens was more common in the days when the privies were in general use, so that when the privy became obsolete there would be extra existing accommodation for the poultry fanciers' flocks.

I have come across a small number of unexpected conversions. One that seemed very enterprising, where the privy was handy

Hen party. (Photo courtesy of Marjorie Campion, Great Asby)

to the house, was a well equipped and comfortably stocked beer store. Another, near the head of the Watendlath Valley, now houses a water purifying plant – a very appropriate new use, somehow; and at Rydal Hall, the scene of Dr Tyson's researches, the privy which Sir Daniel Fleming was overseeing in 1673 now contains a small hydro-electric installation, from which water gushes out into the beck below through the former clearance hole in its back wall.

Our interest in the privies that have begun new careers should not allow us to overlook the others. Throughout Cumbria there are former earth closets that now contain WCs. Some are quite elderly, and would attract the attention of any serious student of the flush; and, of course, they are all at the bottom of the garden, or the yard. There are occasional surprises. At one large house in

78

Multi-purpose privy block handily situated by the beck at Watendlath.

Sir Daniel Fleming's privy at Rydal Hall from across Rydal beck, showing the power of the natural flush in typical Lakeland weather.

Mr W. Airey standing outside the beautifully maintained and still usable privy at Whinfell, Grayrigg.

A National Trust privy in the heart of the Lake District, still in regular use. Note how the field slopes away behind the privy.

High Furness, where there were family and staff closets at opposite ends of the same building, the staff unit was equipped with what is now an old WC, but not the family one. The explanation presumably is that when running water was laid on, the family had entirely new facilities fitted inside, and their old privy was left to decay slowly. Another one which I saw, the one with whitened exterior walls, in the Vale of Newlands, had been recently given both a WC and a washhand basin, matching and attractively designed. The small house does not necessarily have to be a place for penitential meditation.

Other old privies have been carefully preserved by their owners, and these are always in beautiful order. One feels that some of them would qualify as listed buildings without any difficulty. Several privies of this type are to be found on

Relatively recent brick-built privy converted to WC.

properties owned by the National Trust – in trust for the nation, you might say. But the Trust has many and such wide ranging responsibilities that the preservation of its old privies can hardly be high on its list of priorities, nor, one imagines, would the householders involved welcome the creation of a Cumbrian Privy Trail. Everyone has been most kind in allowing Margaret to point her camera in their direction, but once is perhaps enough, and the general wish has been for anonymity to be observed.

Finally, although this category is not a 'conversion', there are pre-flush closets still in use. Some are out in the yard, available 'just in case', like Mr Airey's; others are in regular employment, if only because there is still no mains water connected to the property, and the supply of domestic drinking water is drawn from a small, or uncertain, spring. So there are still places in the county where Sir Daniel Fleming could feel himself at home.

[7]

PERSONAL TALES FROM CUMBRIA

TALES OF TERROR

Imaginative children, faced for the first time with a typical Cumbrian two-holer, however scrupulously maintained, sometimes found it all too much for them. One lad, taken by his parents to the Lake District during the 1940s, just could not bring himself to use the privy, and as a consequence made himself ill and wrecked the family holiday. Jancis Andrews had a similar experience, and recalls the circumstances vividly. On that first day near Nenthead, as recounted in chapter 2, there had been the herd of cattle in the yard. 'On sighting us strangers,' she writes, 'pandemonium broke out. Steam blasting down their cavernous nostrils, eyes rolling madly, their bellowing protests shattering the air, the cows lumbered a full quarter of an inch away in response to Mother's timidly flapping hands. Then they watched us blankly while Mother attempted to make herself understood by repeating "Shoo! Shoo!" Finally, the cow in the outhouse comprehended that Mother wanted it to leave. It blundered to the doorway, paused – and let go a copious, richly pungent, splattering cowpat before rejoining the herd.

'But worse was waiting. I had grown up with toilets that flushed, so it was with horror and consternation that, after timidly circumnavigating the steaming cowpat, I looked down the evil-smelling, black, bottomless pit that Mother insisted was a lavatory – despite the fact that its seat had two holes and there was no flush.

'Giant black rats live down there, I informed her immediately, and if I sat over one of the holes, they would come up and

This family was so delighted when the new flush system was installed around 1930 that they posed outside for this cheerful snapshot.

eat my bottom. Promises that there were positively no rats did not sway me one iota; I knew there were rats down there – razor-toothed, scuttling, with spiky hair and sickly pale tails, their glittering little eyes fixed on the holes above their heads, just waiting.

'And why two holes? Outraged, I assumed this meant I was supposed to chat companionably with Mr. or Miss Stevenson as we did our business side by side.

'Finally, Mother conceded defeat, and we opened the door to find the herd of cows in close formation about the outhouse, patiently waiting in the rain for these peculiar human beings (dainty pastel dresses and shiny patent leather shoes) to show themselves. It took many minutes of increasingly frantic shouts from Mother before a disgusted Mr. Stevenson finally came to escort these dumb townies back to the cottage.

'Mother was sure that nature would force me to use the lavatory eventually. Wrong. My bladder and bowel simply shut down. She enlisted God's and the Stevensons' aid in swearing that there were no rats. I said not a word.

'Ganging together, the adults wielded their ultimate weapon. My older brother Ted (age 9) and even my baby sister Cynthia (5) were not scaredy-cats about a silly little old lavatory, so why couldn't I be like them? Because I wasn't them, I said – an excuse I have repeated over the years, in various forms, in response to one thing or another.

'I don't know when Mother started to panic, but panic she did. I know I felt very uncomfortable by the time Miss Stevenson came to the rescue, lugging a mediaeval French invention – a commode, its wooden seat enclosing a china chamber pot with pink roses smiling around the rim. Chamber pots were familiar.

'I agreed I could co-operate with a commode, so the two women manoeuvred the heavy thing up the ladder staircase and stood it in a corner of the tiniest bedroom.'

There were real rats sometimes. At a few of the farms, especially the ones more given to arable, there were rats 'all over the place', said Peter Bibby. Elsie Youdell, filling out her description of the farm privy as 'horrible', attributed the presence of these undesirable creatures to the circumstance that the privy in question was sited near a beck, and they came up out of the water. Neither were cows the only farmyard residents to strike terror into young hearts, nor Mrs Andrews the only victim. Large birds can seem very menacing to small children. Marjorie Campion recalled the barnyard fowls casting a shadow over otherwise happy visits to her grandmother. To reach the privy she had to cross a yard full of hens and several belligerent cocks, which terrified her to the extent that she was afraid to go on her own. For Mrs Andrews, it was geese, when the family moved from the farm cottage to a house facing onto the village green. This green was grazed by a gander and his harem of geese. 'In his frequent bad moods, he would become a Spitfire (we are thinking back to the 1940s) zooming across the green, his outstretched beak gunning for your fleeing heels, until he'd cornered you in the nettie. Then he wouldn't let you out. Instead, he paced up and down outside the door, his furious honking letting you and the rest of the world know just how much you got on his nerves. If there were no adults available to chase him away, he could keep you imprisoned for hours.'

But even without the hazards created by the local wildlife, visits during the hours of darkness or in specially ferocious Cumbrian weather could be traumatic. If you were only carrying a candle in a bottle, it could easily go out even when the wind was fairly light – and a dark night in the country can be really black. Not long ago the author had considerable trouble in finding his car in an unlit parking area when his electric torch suddenly failed. One enterprising lady told me how she overcame the anxieties attendant on privy calls during dark evenings, at a

Follow the path and you will find it . . .

price. She would give her brother threepence from her pocket money to act as escort, stand sentinel outside and then bring her safely back home. Donald Bowness in Langdale gave himself a degree of reassurance, and perhaps also the feeling that he was keeping up with his friends at a time when his farm had been connected to the electricity supply but remained outside the water mains which served virtually the whole of the village. Now there grew a big yew tree next to the privy at the bottom of the garden. So whenever he had to go during the hours of darkness, he pulled on a certain branch just by the privy door, pretending that this was the light switch. Another boy, Bill McKinney, if plunged into darkness by his oil lamp blowing out, would grope his way back to the kitchen, and postpone the ceremony until driven by desperation to try again.

Not all children were equally resourceful, or phlegmatic. Pairs of sisters would make joint visits for mutual protection, even if this meant being woken from a beauty sleep. Audrey Dent, one of such a pair, wrote: 'It was a major event in the middle of the night if a toilet visit was necessary. I can remember lying awake, dreading the thought, but knowing it was going to be unavoidable, of getting out of my nice warm bed on a cold dark winter's night to face the elements.' The elements could be pretty dreadful in the daytime as well. Mrs Andrews experienced the worst when called to the privy across the green. 'Using the nettie was an endurance marathon involving speed and the ability to survive arctic temperatures. Nothing compares with your bare flesh metamorphosing into ice as, high on Izal (many readers will remember that strong disinfectant which must have perfumed most of the privies in the land fifty years ago), you squat on a frozen wooden seat, a blizzard blasting through the glassless little window and snow drifting under the door.' But the weather, and the movements of assorted animals were not the only causes of unpleasant experiences.

The recollections of Mrs R. P. Leech who went 'into service' not far from Kendal when she left school, still only in her early teens, have haunted her ever since. This particular family was a large one, including four boys. They maintained – at the far end of a paddock, reached by a path which ran past the slaughterhouse (Father Bear was a butcher) – what she describes as a luxurious loo, containing a board pierced by two holes. This in itself was enough to make a young girl who had been brought up with a WC scared of going there at night. What made it so much worse was the boys. Made bold and silly by their superior numbers, they lost no opportunity to play tricks on the poor servant girl, and would even peep through the broken slats at the back of the luxurious installation. The worst thing happened one evening when the parents had gone out. She packed the children off to bed in good time, looking forward to a brief respite from persecution. It was a pleasant summer evening so she strolled into the garden at the front of the house, where she was 'enjoying a laugh and a chat with the local boys, when there was a sudden deluge. The young imps had opened a window and emptied the "goes-under" on us.' Very soon after, she moved to another, and sedater, place. This recalls the probably not unique story of the lady who emptied the chamber pot over her husband whenever he came home drunk, in hopes of curing him. There is no information on the success of the treatment, or whether the marriage drifted onto the rocks.

THE DOCTOR'S STORY

A really horrifying story was told to me by Tobias Atkinson, who had it from the doctor in question. He, the doctor, was called out on a bitterly cold night to a remote cottage. The month was January, the moon steely bright. The girl, he had been told, had suffered a severe haemorrhage, her condition was serious. As he drove his trap along the rough, unmade track he could only wonder what he should find at the end of the road. Once arrived, his suspicions were confirmed. The girl, deathly pale, and in obvious distress, could not deny what to him were unmistakable signs of childbirth. 'But, the child?' he asked, with a renewed fear in his heart. The poor girl had been so terrified of the consequences of giving birth to a child out of wedlock that she had gone to great pains – literally – to conceal her condition, and had now produced the baby without help from anyone. 'But, the child?' he repeated.

Then she confessed that she had put it straight down the hole in the privy. By the light of that unfeeling moon, the doctor rushed out to the small house, where he found that he was able to retrieve the tiny body, after manhandling the huge slate away

91

from the clearance hole on the ashpit side of the building. Bearing it inside, protected by his greatcoat, he sat by the cottage fire with the baby, blue already from exposure, on his lap. Calling for warm water and a clean cloth, he began gently to wash it and, as he did so, the warmth and the careful massage slowly revived the flickering flame of life. Meanwhile he did his best to convince the girl that her guilty conscience was as nothing compared to her responsibility for the life that was now hanging in the balance at her side.

The story has a happy ending. The girl, under his continuing care, mothered her firstborn, who grew up to be a fine, strapping lad, able, eventually, to support her in her old age.

A MISCELLANY OF TALES

In general, people's memories have retained the more ludicrous or, in retrospect, mildly humorous incidents associated with the privies of yesterday. A good example is the misadventure of the young lady who had been invited to a 21st birthday party at a farm way out on the moors in North Cumbria. Realising, well into the proceedings, that she would have to pay a call, she whispered her need discreetly into a friendly ear. An electric torch was quicky found, directions for the journey given, and she set out bravely into the darkness. All went well until she had actually found her way into the privy, which was a two-holer. There, not seeing any convenient shelf or bracket, she placed the torch, one of the cylindrical sort, on the wooden bench, and, of course, when she was in no position to grab it, the wretched thing rolled into the vacant hole. Wisely, she made no attempt to fish it out, but then had some ado finding her way back to the party, where she became briefly the centre of embarrassed attention, quite upstaging the real star of the evening.

Seating arrangements at the National Trust farm in Yewdale. This privy is still usable.

The incident had probably come as no surprise to the regulars. The seat boards in some of these old privies bore no resemblance to a billiard table. There was a notoriously sloping one at a farm just outside Coniston, to which Elsie Bowness moved after her wedding. All the workmen who came to the place knew about it, and would probably have been disappointed if it had been altered. After all, it had been like this for longer than anybody could remember, and once you got the knack of balancing, you were alright. Not so, however, if you were using the installation for the first time, and if you were aunt to the newly married farmer's wife, who had only recently come to live at the farm, which, it should be noted, overlooked one of our more splendid lakes. Aunty had not been told that the board was so slanting that if you didn't hold on, you would slip off. She was eloquent on the subject when she returned to the kitchen: 'I thought, surely, I'se gan back into t'lake,' she said, just as an introductory shot. And she never went to that privy again without making the same observation. But as the farmer's wife said to me, as if excusing the poor little privy, 'it was very old'.

Sisters often found the small house a haven of quiet, away from the hurly-burly of family life in a perhaps overcrowded cottage. 'It was our only opportunity', wrote Margaret Procter, looking back on her childhood in the Rusland Valley, 'to plan and plot our day.' And, note, strict protocol was observed – the younger sister had to occupy the smaller hole.

One of our informants told us in a quite matter-of-fact way how she spent many hours alone in the privy before she was old

Clearance hole for privy in the Coppermines Valley, just above a tiny stream that runs down behind the block.

enough to go to school. Not a case of neglect, or cruelty, I hasten to add, but an illustration of the problems that mothers had to cope with not so many years ago. She had to take her little boy to the village school when he reached the age of five – but the school was a forty minute walk away. So twice a day, whatever the weather, she had to fit the school walk into her household routine. A three year old girl couldn't walk that far, and there was no-one nearby to keep an eye on the baby, so she popped her in the privy, no doubt having checked that the hole lid was securely fastened. At least, she couldn't come to any harm from the fire, or the stairs, if she was in the small house. 'But it did seem such a long time, especially when it was dark.' Fortunately for all concerned, the Local Education Authority began to operate a school taxi service at precisely the time when she would have had to exchange the long imprisonment for the long walk.

From Mrs C. Moore comes the tale of the sick Scot. When her mother, Laura Pinch, was a child the family lived in Oxenholme, on one of the main north-south lines of communication. In the days before 1914 it was not uncommon for travelling pedlars or chapmen to call on their way through, offering their wares to the villagers. The Scottish gentleman, then, had called, and it was apparent to Mrs Pinch's mother that he was rather the worse for drink. She was not altogether surprised, therefore, when he asked, on taking his leave, whether he might use the privy at the far end of the yard. 'She, being a lady,' writes Mrs Moore, 'and of a generous and caring nature, immediately agreed and indicated the way. After some time, which my Mother said seemed like half an hour, but in reality would only be about fifteen minutes, the family thought they should investigate. They crept across the yard and approached the privy's open door to see our Scottish friend seated over one hole with

General view of the privy at a big farm near Farleton. Ashes were piled in the
angle formed by the wall and the building.

his head down the adjacent hole, vomiting, and exclaiming,
"Sweet Edinburgh, I smell thee noo!"'

Especially in good weather, it was quite usual not to bother
closing the privy door, and thereby a certain lady in an isolated
Furness hamlet was seriously embarrassed one summer morning. Again we go back through the years to the time when 'club
chaps', as we used to call the agents of the little local sick and
burial societies, came regularly to collect a family's small contri-
butions. It so fell out that a new man had taken over this particular round, and it was his first visit to the scattered hamlet.
Knocking on the kitchen door, he raised only the small daughter
of the house, who answered in reply to his enquiry whether

Mother was in, that she was just down the garden, and he would find her there. In all innocence he set off in the direction indicated to confront the open door of the privy just beyond a big bank of rose bushes, and Mother, at the bottom of the garden indeed, but seated upon the throne. Delicacy prompted an apologetic and hasty retreat.

This sense of delicacy did not always wait for some untoward event to upset people's susceptibilities. There was the unmarried vicar, for instance, who had a new privy set up 'for the use of his maids', thereby avoiding any risk of encountering them on his way to or from the little house.

It must not be supposed that such a degree of refined sensibility was invariably the norm. The miners and quarrymen had to shift for themselves as best they could, and a century ago there were far more of them at the workplaces than there are on today's remaining sites. The end of the quarry tip was a favoured place to go, as being reasonably quiet and not likely to upset anyone else. Most of them would prudently keep a square of paper in some handy pocket. (The more feckless are said to have been content with bracken fronds, but this could only have been so in summer.) But this primitive, uncomfortable and sometimes dangerous venue did not always meet with official approval. It is said of one quarry owner at Broughton Moor that he called the workforce together and observed that he did not wish to see all those gingerbread papers scattered over the end of the tip. He does not seem to have gone on from there to have a simple privy constructed. Yet there must have been plenty of suitable stone ready to hand.

We have already seen how the men who emptied the privies were liable to sing loudly as they went about their work. Maybe there was something about a privy, like a bathroom, that

Pair of quite modern privies separated by a rose bush in Monk Coniston.

encouraged song. Perhaps the voice resonated well, or it was a means of passing the time, or of keeping one's spirits up in a lonesome and possibly dark situation. Tobias Atkinson told me a delightful story, from his childhood days in Holme, about an old lady who lived alone in a small cottage in one of our villages. Other members of the family lived not too far away, and they kept an eye on her by helping with the more onerous domestic tasks. So every Monday morning one of her nephews would come to the cottage. He was a nice young chap, but not too bright, which was the reason why he did not do a full-time job, but he was perfectly able to see Aunty through the hard work of washing day. She certainly appreciated both his help and his cheerful if sometimes inconsequential company, and would frequently have a laugh with the neighbours who had overheard him singing in the privy. She herself was Church, but he was Chapel, and she said she always knew what hymns they had sung the day before by the end of his weekly recital.

Some of the men to whom I have spoken have told me of the opportunities given for mischievous diversion by the old privies. We should bear in mind that it was not difficult to remove the flagstone which closed the clearance opening at the back, and that usually the ground fell away on this side of the small house. Your average naughty boy, therefore, William Airey of Grayrigg told me, could arm himself with a good stout nettle fixed to the end of a stick (let's hope he stung himself setting up the device!), or a gorse branch, similarly extended. Then he would lurk in wait for an older sister or other suitable victim. Once comfortably enthroned, the occupant would be subjected to sting or prickle treatment, operated by remote control from somewhere outside at the back. One lad looked back to the day when he tickled the teacher's bottom as one of the highlights of his primary school career. Here, of course, there would be the added spice of danger should the culprit be brought to book.

The corrugated iron, or 'tin sheet', mode of privy construction lent itself to another lively practical joke, recounted by Grace Sloan. The new servant girl at a farm near Lamplugh was terrified out of her mind by a young man who had made a stealthy approach to the back of the privy, and then made a fearful racket by running a stout stick over the corrugations.

Another favourite form of torture was the burning newspaper. This was more difficult to accomplish in what may be termed landlocked privies, but could be highly effective when applied to drops over, or immediately alongside, water. For equipment, you needed a flat piece of wood with a nail driven in centrally at one end, a good length of string, newspaper and matches.

The privy down the field (literally). This privy is newer than the very primitive house which it served within living memory. The former dwelling has been converted into a sheep shelter.

Having attached your board to the string by means of the nail, you crumpled as much newspaper as you dared, set it upon the board, and lowered the fireship gently into the water. It remained only to apply a match, and then by means of the string you could bring the burning paper to a halt immediately below the hole over which your victim was seated. A quick and indignant exit could be guaranteed. The privies themselves were so strongly built that there was minimal risk of setting the whole place on fire, though I was told of this happening once.

The final story in this section, told by Mr J. E. Hellen, relates to a farm situated on the moorland fringe. As sometimes happens, there were more sons in the family than the farm could support as they grew up, and one of them decided to join the army. Since they were a closely knit family, he kept in regular touch with home through letters exchanged with Mother. In the course of time he was posted overseas. Soon afterwards the family got a grant to install running water and, with it, indoor sanitation. This news was passed to him by Mother, whose delight increased once everything was in place. No need for any more of those cold trips down the yard – the privy was on the far side, opposite the back door, and had been a wonderfully draughty place because it was one of the kind where the door comes to an end four inches or more above the ground. However, after several more letters had been exchanged, a note of anxiety began to creep into Mother's bulletins from home. She could not persuade Father to forsake the practice of a lifetime, and abandon the old privy.

The lad loved his mother, and the thought of her being upset or embarrassed by this disturbed him. So when, some months later, he was able to return home for a spell of leave he said to her as they stood outside the kitchen door on his arrival, 'And have you broken Father off from using that place yet?' – waving a hand in the direction of the privy. She had to admit failure. 'I'll soon cure this,' he said, and rummaged in the kitbag that lay at his feet. He had smuggled a practice hand grenade out of the camp, anticipating just such a contingency. Reaching it out, he pulled the pin away, and bowled the grenade across the yard. Under the door it rolled, then went off with an explosion that blew out the door and brought the roof down. Turning to Mother with pride, he was aghast to see her eyes full of tears. 'You shouldn't have done that,' she wailed – 'Your Father's in there!' But even as she spoke, a figure limped out, jacket torn, cap askew, face covered in dust. 'By gow,' he muttered, rubbing his eyes as he approached the kitchen door, 'if that's what two spoonfuls of castor oil can do, why does anybody bother with dynamite . . .'

[8]

PRIVIES – THEM WAS THE DAYS?

On the debit side of a Cumbrian privy balance sheet, the weather must take pride of place. So often the journey through the garden, perhaps involving short flights of rough stone steps, or across a yard occupied by farm animals, was made additionally unpleasant or hazardous by rain, snow, cold winds or darkness – three out of the four could be, and not infrequently were, operating simultaneously.

Next, we must take into account the regular sheer hard work that went into keeping the little house clean and tidy, such as carrying out the water for scrubbing, ensuring an adequate supply of ashes, and so on. In this context, however, the privy chores simply took their place with all the other inescapable domestic tasks like washing and ironing, which were equally demanding physically and more time-consuming – so whilst ladies in particular may shudder as they think back to putting scrubbing brush to privy flags, this must have been no worse than bending over a dolly tub every Monday morning.

Younger children and elderly or disabled adults suffered most from the situation of the privy. In particular, we should not underestimate the terror created by total darkness, even in persons brought up in places where there was no exterior lighting of any kind. Yet few households were without a commode, and all kept chamber pots, the use of which must have alleviated the perils and discomforts of the long trek.

Then, the earth closet was more open to the kind of elementary practical joke which appeals especially to small boys. But, even for the victims, this treatment must have been intermittent . . . mustn't it?

There is also the question of how the multi-hole units were used. My impression is that this arrangement was intended primarily to match the different sizes of the users, and that it was seldom the practice for two persons to crowd into the privy at the same time. The second hole, of course, was available for emergencies, or for a parent accompanying a small child at toilet training time, or even later, if the youngster was of a nervous disposition. Not that this situation arose very often. Country children are early made aware of all the natural functions of mammals, and tend to have an unselfconscious attitude to these matters as applied to themselves.

So far we have been thinking of the rural areas where the number of persons using any given privy was not large, and where there was plenty of room to dispose of the contents, however distasteful the task of disposal might be for the person who had to do it. The towns were different (or, for that matter, the privies of country families who were not careful about maintenance, and where there were a great many children). Over-use and under-cleaning created fearful problems, and materially spoiled the quality of life for thousands of people. We are fortunate that the disease and squalor associated for generations with the privies in the overcrowded parts of our towns are a thing of the past.

Distance, they say, lends enchantment, and this seems to be true of many of the memories which have been shared with me. But they can't all be put down to a romantic nostalgia. The small house provided a quiet retreat. The pile of newspapers and magazines at the end of the bench was ostensibly to provide an emergency supply of paper if the official cutter had skimped her work the previous Saturday. But everyone knew there was another use for them. They gave the opportunity for a quiet read and sit-down, to break up a long morning of hard work – or, no doubt, just for a quiet read. Mrs Atkinson made this

The sort of place where a person might sit listening to the birds on a May morning, at a farm in High Furness.

point very clearly. Having moved to a Lakeland farm,and made her first acquaintance with an earth privy, one of the first things she did was to fix a toilet roll to the wall. 'But', she wrote, 'that didn't stop the pile of old newspapers being stacked neatly in the corner, and I soon discovered the reason. There's no rush or scramble in the country to catch a certain bus or train, so instead of sitting there fuming about all the 101 jobs you have to do, what could be more relaxing and rewarding than browsing through a batch of old newspapers, picking out those articles you missed before, whilst letting nature take her course?'

'Another bonus', Mrs Atkinson continues, 'is that our little house is within earshot of an orchestral concert provided by blackbirds, thrushes and robins, perched in nearby trees . . . A seat in the centre of the dress circle for the concert.' Indeed Edith Bowness commented that 'throne' was a very apt word to describe the privy seat – 'You felt quite regal, sitting up there,' she said. It is easy to understand why, in the better weather, people didn't bother to shut the door. Quite apart from the birds and the garden flowers, many of these Cumbrian loos had superb views over valley, moor or mountain, whereas farm or cottage kitchens often merely looked onto a yard or out-buildings.

In more strictly practical terms, several folk commented that the wooden bench was a more satisfactory seat than the plastic ring which tops most of our contemporary WCs. There is also the question of smell, which is remarkably absent from nearly all the recollections. The ashes and the superb ventilation no doubt helped in this connection, quite apart from the overpow-ering effect of the ubiquitous Izal, or Jeyes' Fluid. There must have been what Bertie Wooster would have described as a 'nif' from time to time, perhaps related to the strength and direction of the wind. But which indoor WC is completely odourless? One lady observed that she was immediately conscious of the

Across the garden, a Farleton farm privy.

proximity of the loos in hotels or other public buildings; and Mrs Andrews makes the same point, with her usual vigour: 'Visits to the toilet', she writes, 'are now as near as the next room, and will be warm, hygienic and free from attack. And instead of the muscular Izal standing guard in a blizzard-blasted corner, there will probably be a pastel-coloured plastic flower simpering on the wall, and coyly offering something like Meadowsweet Bathroom Freshener.'

The people whose privy emptied into a beck would have no problems with smells or clearance. But what about the folk who lived downstream? The answer is that very seldom would there be any neighbours downstream, or up, and that drinking water came from a separate spring, anyway! But I was reassured further by being told of an old Dalesman's test of drinkability, when out on his business among the fells. 'If you are desperate for a drink,' he said, 'go upstream for 200 yards from where you are. If the beck is not blocked by a dead sheep, or other obnoxious material for that distance, it will be safe to return to your starting point, and drink from there.' It is interesting in this context that the 17th-century Manor Court records of Torver show that there was little trouble with faulty privies, but quite a lot of concern about watercourses being blocked by dead animals.

To conclude the credit side of the privy balance sheet, we should note how in the scattered rural communities the earth closet was a perfectly acceptable feature of a sustainable 'green' lifestyle. The natural waste products were returned to the soil and acted as a fertilizer to produce better crops for both human and animal consumption. So the privy that cleared itself into the farm midden could be regarded as superior to any of the trouble-free, beck-flushed installations. All the same, it must have been exciting, after heavy rain, to sit perched over a raging torrent. Mrs Andrews is right again when she observes that toilet visits are now much duller, and that the tameness of modern bathrooms leaves the present generation with 'no character-building sanitation adventures to boast about to their children and grandchildren, which is something I can do to mine.'

[9]

THE POOR LITTLE HAS-BEEN

I'm a 'privy' at the bottom of the garden
All purpose built and private as can be
An intruder when I'm occupied must ask for pardon
Although there's room enough in here for three

I think I'm something special, though I wouldn't say I'm smart
My walls are painted white and rather bare
I'm just an ordinary little building from others set apart
But when you're desperate and you need me I am there

Should you be sitting comfortable and cosy
And you hear a noise behind which makes you quake
Don't worry it's not someone being nosey
It's old Tom who's come to clean me with his rake

Old Tom's the man who, monthly, calls to take away my load
With his job well done, I couldn't feel much cleaner
Oh! It's good to hear his cart wheels on the road
And the fields around are definitely greener!

I've a secret that perhaps I shouldn't tell you
But I will because, you see, it boosts my pride
If the menfolk through the day get tired, as they do
I'm the quiet little haven where they hide

One day a week my mistress goes quite crazy
She attacks me like the waves upon a beach
When she's finished I am whiter than a daisy
Through her scrubbing and her scouring with the bleach

Today I heard a very tragic story
I do believe we're going to get the push
Yes, we at last are giving up our glory
To a new sophisticated toilet that will flush

BUT

When the plumbing's all gone wrong
Or the summer drought is long
And the water isn't flushing as it should
Ah! then you'll all be wishing that we hadn't gone for good

**Audrey Dent
Bolton, Cumbria**

A PRIVY BY ANY OTHER NAME

Closet, dry close, earth closet
Down (or up) the garden
   (or yard)
Garderobe
Houses of Parliament
Klondike
Latrine
Lavatory
Little house, small house
Long drop

Loo
Netty/nettie
One-holer, two-holer,
   three-holer
Reading room
Reredorter (mediaeval
   abbeys)
The necessary (house)
The throne room